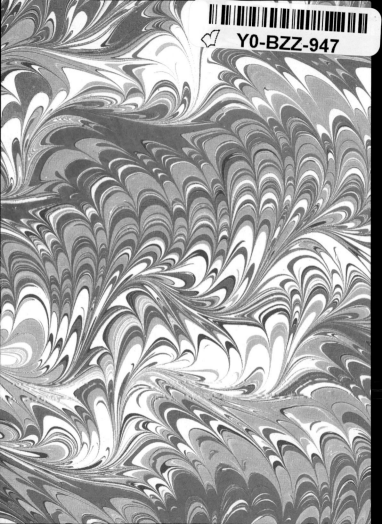

HOLD A PROBLEM IN
YOUR MIND

OPEN THIS BOOK TO
ANY PAGE

AND THERE WILL BE
YOUR ANSWER.

BEGIN IT NOW

Other books by Susan Hayward

A GUIDE FOR THE ADVANCED SOUL
Pocket Edition - 0 9577025 1 5

BAG OF JEWELS
Pocket Edition - 0 9577025 3 1

BEING - REMINDERS FROM THE GODS
Hardcover - 0 9590439 8 5

YOU HAVE A PURPOSE

BEGIN IT NOW

SUSAN HAYWARD

HAYWARD
BOOKS

HAYWARD BOOKS
PO BOX 193 AVALON NSW 2107
AUSTRALIA
email: letbe@ozemail.com.au

First published in Hardcover Sept 1987
Pocket edition October 1999

BEGIN IT NOW
Copyright © 1987 Susan Hayward
All rights reserved.

Quotations calligraphy by Susan Hayward
Chinese calligraphy by Amy Huang
Jacket calligraphy by Dave Wood
Endpapers by Margo Snape
Produced by Phoenix Offset, HK.

ISBN 0 9577025 2 3

International Distribution: AUST: HarperCollins, NZ:
HarperCollins, UK: Tiptree Distribution (TBS) USA: Words,
Bookpeople,New Leaf, Ingrams. SA: Alternate Books,
Mail Order: Amazon.com, B&N.com, Borders.com.

For my Dad - whose visionary ideals and courageous plans inspired me to live my life as a daring adventure.

Acknowledgments

I would like to thank all the contributors to this book who gave so much more than their professional skills along the way:

Amy huang for your Chinese calligraphy. Each quote is embellished by her ideograms, which encompass the meaning of those words beautifully.

Dave Wood for your inspiring jacket design; to Margo Snape for your endpaper marbling (and valuable advice); and to John Bull for refining the artwork on a last minute deadline!

Thank you also to my friends who let me borrow your books, and for all your encouragement. To Mark Brodbeck my appreciation for your time and talent in taking my photograph. And to my loving husband, whose unfailing support was always there.

And lastly, to the greatest and noblest spirits who have lived on this planet, whatever the time or place, many of whom grace the pages of this book.

Introduction

Just for a moment, imagine yourself as a master of the universe: you have the ability to create something that has never existed or been done before. Be outrageous in your thinking and envision what you most want now.

In fact, you have this Power in you - it is the birthright and potentiality of every human being. Our thoughts and imaginations are the only real limits to our possibilities. Once you have a clear vision of what you want - focussing on the result and not the means - the natural play of Universal forces lead you to the accomplishment of that goal. Your dream can be made a reality by taking it seriously.

Begin It Now is about living your life to the ultimate: taking your ideas and aspirations, acting on them, seeing them through to success, and not giving up when the quest gets challenging.

Recall those times when your motivation is at its lowest ebb, when you feel your project has lost all meaning, holds no interest anymore, and there is the possibility of giving up, giving it all away. We often encounter stumbling blocks and challenges on the path to success - but they are only there to learn from, to show you a new way!

This book is for those times; to encourage and help you to change that direction, and be open to changing your ideas and possible futures. At your most confusing and directionless times, focus your attention on your difficulty or stumbling block. Open this book to any page at random and there will be your answer. What you will read are pearls of wisdom from great visionaries, thinkers, spiritual teachers, corporate leaders, poets, scientists, and statesmen - from the past and our contemporaries. These men and women have dared to go beyond the accepted limits of what is possible. They have accessed a greater part of their abilities by being unlimited in their thinking, choosing to go beyond the 'normal'. They have achieved mastery, and have a loftier perspective on life. Life for them is a flame, it is explosive!

But following in the footsteps of those great teachers will not give you 'understanding,' unless you are aready to personally experience their insights by **taking action.**

Often the one thing we really want to do in life is not begun because of the fear we feel just thinking about it. The greatest growth and personal development is achieved through taking a risk and facing those fears. The time you least feel like starting something is precisely the time to *Begin It*

Now. You may not have a clear idea of what you want to do, or even if you are doing exactly what you THINK you want to do. But just the physical act of **beginning** will create the momentum and energy to develop towards your greatest accomplishments. Be disciplined, and give enthusiasm to whatever you do. Have faith in yourself, be tenacious, have high personal standards and integrity, and your life will blossom : You will resonate at a higher frequency, thereby increasing your energy and manifestation of desires.

I took the risk in publishing, writing and distributing my first book *A Guide For The Advanced Soul*, which is now a successful seller - without any previous knowledge of this process. The wisdom and spiritual principles gained from the experience has enabled me to create this sequel *Begin It Now*. I want to encourage others to take that same risk, to be unlimited, to fulfill their unique destiny, to be creative in their lifestyle, and to open their consciousness to greater levels of life and being.

We are here to experience life. To be fulfilled, to be happy, to be joyful in your life, this **is** your destiny. Take your dream seriously - You are here to become the best you can be.

Susan Hayward

專

Until one is committed, there is hesitancy, the chance to draw back, always ineffectiveness.

Concerning all acts of initiative (and creation), there is one elementary truth, the ignorance of which kills countless ideas and splendid plans: that the moment one definitely commits oneself, then Providence moves too.

All sorts of things occur to help one that would never otherwise have occurred. A whole stream of events issues from the decision, raising in one's favour all manner of unforeseen incidents and meetings and material assistance, which no man could have dreamed would have come his way.

W.H. MURRAY

Whatever
you can do
Or dream you can,
Begin it.
Boldness has genius,
power and magic
in it.
BEGIN IT NOW.

GOETHE

知

What would
you attempt to do
    if you knew
        you could not fail?

DR ROBERT SCHULLER

幻

Imagination
is more
important
than
knowledge.

ALBERT EINSTEIN

Come to the edge, he said
They said: We are afraid
Come to the edge, he said
They came.
he pushed them...
and they flew.

GUILLAUME APOLLINAIRE

Every great
and commanding movement
in the annals of the world
is the triumph
of enthusiasm.

Nothing great
was ever achieved
without it.

RALPH WALDO EMERSON

疑

Nothing
is so exhausting
as indecision,

and nothing
is so futile.

BERTRAND RUSSELL

The only way
to discover
the limits
of the possible
is to go
beyond them,
to the impossible.

ARTHUR C. CLARKE

One of
the most important
results
you can bring
into the world

Is the you
that you
really want to be.

ROBERT FRITZ

Everyone has talent.

What is rare
is the courage
to follow
the talent
to the dark place
where it leads.

ERICA JONG

Do not be afraid
   of enthusiasm.

You need it.

You can do nothing
   effectually
      without it.

FRANÇOIS GUIZOT

Often the difference
between a successful man
and a failure
is not one's better abilities
or ideas,
but the courage that one has
to bet on his ideas,
to take a calculated risk
and to act.

MAXWELL MALTZ

Each time you accept a
thought that is greater than what
you have accepted as your standard,
that thought activates yet
another part of your brain into
purposeful use. Each time you
do that, the greater thought will
offer itself as a carrier to expand
your reasoning from that point.

That will activate other
portions of your brain for more
thought, for more receiving, for
more knowing.

You know, it is very simple
to be a genius. All you have to do
is think for yourself.

RAMTHA

There are risks
and costs
to a programme
of action,

but they are far less
than the long-range
risks and costs
of comfortable
inaction.

JOHN F. KENNEDY

步

Stopping, starting,
being diverted,
becoming impatient,
is indirect and the
least successful means
of accomplishment.

Nothing moves
but by degrees.

Each step forward,
no matter how small,
is one step less
that has to be taken.

BRIAN ADAMS

It is a commonplace
observation
   that work expands
   so as to fill
   the time available
for its completion.

C. NORTHCOTE PARKINSON

儋

Without deviation,
progress
is not
possible.

FRANK ZAPPA

Anyone who lives
within his means
suffers
from a lack
of
imagination.

LIONEL STANDER

What the hell–
you might be right,
you might be wrong...
but don't just avoid.

KATHARINE HEPBURN

The method
of the enterprising
is to plan with audacity,
and execute with vigour;
to sketch out
a map of possibilities;
And then
to treat them
as probabilities.

BOVEE

Victory
belongs
to the most
persevering.

NAPOLEON

One of the best ways to properly evaluate and adapt to the many environmental stresses of life is to simply view them as normal.

The adversity and failures in our lives, if adapted to and viewed as normal corrective feedback to use to get back on target, serve to develop in us an immunity against anxiety, depression, and the adverse responses to stress.

Instead of tackling the most important priorities that would make us successful and effective in life, we prefer the path of least resistance and do things simply that will relieve our tension, such as shuffling papers and majoring in minors.

DENIS WAITLEY

Since the mind is a specific biocomputer, it needs specific instructions and directions.

The reason most people never reach their goals is that they don't define them, learn about them, or ever seriously consider them as believable or achievable.

In other words, they set them up (to lose).

Winners can tell you where they are going, what they plan to do along the way, and who will be sharing the adventure with them.

DENIS WAITLEY

Procrastination
is the thief
of time.

EDWARD YOUNG

As long as you have a cloister-
ed mind and live and think accord-
ing to social consciousness, you
will never venture into the
unknown or contemplate the
possibility of greater realities
for fear that it will mean change.

And certainly it will, because
there will be more to see, to understand, and to be a part of, than
there was before in a tidy world
that lives and dies. As long as you
accept only those limited thoughts
that have been bred into you, you
will never activate greater portions
of your brain to receive and
experience any thought other
than what you have faced every
day of your existence.

RAMTHA

折

The life-spirit
and energy
which contribute
to the mastery
of the creative process
can never
be fully engaged
by a commitment
to a compromise.

ROBERT FRITZ

When a tough, challenging job
is to be done, I look for a person
who possesses an enthusiasm
and optimism for life.
Who makes a zestful
confident attack on his
daily problems,
One who shows courage and
imagination,
Who pins down his buoyant
spirit with careful planning
and hard work,
but says,
'This may be tough,
but it can be licked'.

HENRY J KAISER

Life is either
a daring adventure
or nothing.

Security does not exist in nature,
nor do the children of men
as a whole experience it.

Avoiding danger
is no safer
in the long run
than exposure.

HELEN KELLER

The message seems to be that life is made up of winners and losers. If you are not number one or in the top five you have failed.

There doesn't seem to be any reward for simply succeeding at the level of doing one's best.

Success is how you collect your minutes. You spend millions of minutes to reach one triumph, one moment, then you spend maybe a thousand minutes enjoying it. If you are unhappy through those millions of minutes, what good are the thousand minutes of triumph? It doesn't equate.

CONT'D

Life is made up of small pleasures.

happiness is made up of those tiny successes. The big ones come too infrequently.

If you don't have all of those zillions of tiny successes, the big ones don't mean anything.

NORMAN LEAR

The shortest way
to do many things
is to do
only one thing
at once.

SAMUEL SMILES

People are always
blaming circumstances
for what they are.

I do not believe
in circumstances.

The people who get on
in this world are the people
who get up and look for the
circumstances they want,
and if they cannot find them,
make them.

GEORGE BERNARD SHAW

Follow your heart, your
dreams, your desires. Do what
your soul calls you to do, whatever
it is, and allow it to be finished;
then you will go on to another
adventure.

You will never be judged—
unless you accept the judgement
of those around you.

And if you accept their
judgement, it is only your will to
do so—for the experience.

RAMTHA

Creativity represents
a miraculous coming together
of the uninhibited energy
of the child

With its apparent
opposite and enemy,

the sense of order
imposed on the disciplined
adult intelligence.

NORMAN PODHORETZ

We are not here just to survive
and live long...

We are here to live and know life
in its multi-dimensions
to know life in its richness,
in all its variety.

And when a man lives multi-
dimensionally, explores all
possibilities available,
never shrinks back
from any challenge,
Goes, rushes to it, welcomes it,
rises to the occasion
then life becomes a flame,
life blooms.

BHAGWAN SHREE RAJNEESH

It seems that
you are happy
and successful in life
if you are doing your thing,
you know specifically what your
thing is, and that which you are
doing earns you the respect
of other people, because
what you are doing
benefits other people
as well as
yourself.

DENIS WAITLEY

If I had a formula
for bypassing trouble,
I would not pass it round.
Trouble creates a capacity
to handle it.

I don't embrace trouble;
that's as bad as treating it
as an enemy.

But I do say meet it as
a friend, for you'll see
a lot of it and had better be
on speaking terms with it.

OLIVER WENDELL HOLMES

When people say to me:
   'how do you do so many things?'
I often answer them, without
meaning to be cruel:
   'how do you do so little?'

It seems to me that people
   have vast potential.
Most people can do extraordinary
things if they have the
confidence or take the risks.
   Yet most people don't.
   They sit in front of the telly
   and treat life as if it
   goes on forever.

PHILLIP ADAMS

He who has
    begun his task
has half done it.

HORACE

Begin difficult things
    while they are easy,
        Do great things
            when they are small.
The difficult things of the world
    must once have been easy;
The great things
    must once have been small ...
A thousand mile journey
    begins with
        one step.

LAO-TSE

With discipline
comes organisation,
strength of purpose,
determination and success.

Without discipline
there is disorganisation,
confusion and failure.

Carry each job to completion.
To do this is to avoid confusion.

Back your organised effort
with enthusiasm,
faith and integrity.

BRIAN ADAMS

Don't be afraid
to take a big step
if one is indicated.

You can't cross a chasm
in two small jumps.

DAVID LLOYD GEORGE

There are many who are living far below their possibilities because they are continually handing over their individualities to others.

Do you want to be a power in the world? Then be yourself.

Be true to the highest within your soul and then allow yourself to be governed by no customs or conventionalities or arbitrary man-made rules that are not founded on principle.

RALPH WALDO TRINE

You didn't think when you got up this morning that this would be the day your life would change, did you? But it's going to happen because the only thing that stands between you and grand success in living are these two things: Getting started and never quitting! You can solve your biggest problem by getting started, right here and now.

ROBERT H SCHULLER

理

Ideas by themselves
cannot produce
change of being;

Your effort must go
in the right direction.

And one must correspond
to the other.

P.D. OUSPENSKY
G.I. GURDJIEFF

One of the important things to remember is to use your imagination to the hilt. This is your intuitive force telling you to soar, and the more you use it the higher you will go with it. Most people don't have it. They get caught up in movies, T.V. and beer and get accustomed to habit. Habit is a very bad thing even if it's a good habit. For instance, in going to work every day, go by a different route, because adventure may be just around the corner. If you think anything can happen, it will.

Be an individual; think with your imagination.

GURU RHH

I have learned more
from my mistakes
than from
my successes.

SIR HUMPHRY DAVY

Procrastination is the fear of success. People procrastinate because they are afraid of the success that they know will result if they move ahead now.

Because success is heavy, carries a responsibility with it, and requires an individual to continue to set an example, it is much easier to procrastinate and live on the 'someday I'll' philosophy.

Winners don't live their lives in the future, safely out of sight.

They set goals in the specific, foreseeable future, which gives their everyday activities richness and purpose.

DENIS WAITLEY

You always need committees, because that's where people share their knowledge and intentions. But when committees replace individuals... then productivity begins to decline.

Nothing stands still in this world. I like to go duck hunting, where constant movement and change are facts of life. You can aim at a duck and get it in your sights, but the duck is always moving. In order to hit the duck, you have to move your gun. But a committee faced with a major decision can't always move as quickly as the events it's trying to respond to. By the time the committee is ready to shoot, the duck has flown away.

LEE IACOCCA

Some men
see things
as they are
and say why?

I dream things
that never were
and say
'Why not?'

R.F. KENNEDY

We learn wisdom
from failure
much more than
from success;
We often discover
what will do,
by finding out
what will not do;

and probably he who
never made a mistake
never made
a discovery.

SAMUEL SMILES

The only reason someone is a genius, and knows things you do not know, is because he has opened his mind to contemplate the what-ifs, the outrageous thoughts, the thoughts of brilliance that go beyond the limited thinking of man. He has allowed himself to entertain and reason with these thoughts, whereas you have rejected them.

If any one thing can be conceived or pondered, it exists; for whatever is dreamed or imagined is already within the realm of existence. That is how all of creation came into existence.

RAMTHA

People who feel
they have to do things
usually forfeit
many available options
and alternatives

and lose control
of their lives
in the process.

DENIS WAITLEY

Pavlov's advice on how to succeed– 'Passion and gradualness'. Even in those areas where we have already developed a high degree of skill, it sometimes helps to drop back, lower our sights a bit, and practice with a feeling of ease.

This is especially true when one reaches a 'sticking point' in progress, where effort for additional progress is unavailing.

Continually straining to beyond the 'sticking point' is likely to develop undesirable 'feeling habits' of strain, difficulty, effort.

MAXWELL MALTZ

The block of granite
which was an obstacle
in the pathway
of the weak,

became a stepping-stone
in the pathway
of the strong.

THOMAS CARLYLE

Experience
  helps build momentum.
Build momentum rather
  than problem solving in
  going after goals.
Look for new ways to build
  momentum - experiment
  and seek out challenges.
Challenge helps build
  momentum, but not
  reaching too far at first.

ROBERT FRITZ

Time is an invention.

Now is a reality.

So much creativity is happening
for the simple reason that we
have withdrawn ourselves
from past and future.

Our whole energy remains
blocked, either in the past
or in the future.

When you withdraw
all your energy from past
and future
a tremendous explosion happens.

That explosion is creativity.

BHAGWAN SHREE RAJNEESH

I never
take counsel
of my fears.

GENERAL GEORGE PATTON

階

The rung of a ladder
was never meant to rest upon,
but only to hold a man's foot
long enough to enable him
to put the other
somewhat higher.

THOMAS HENRY HUXLEY

People who fail to achieve their goals usually get stopped by frustration.

They allow frustration to keep them from taking the necessary actions that would support them in achieving their desire.

You get through this roadblock by plowing through frustration, taking each setback as feedback you can learn from, and pushing ahead.

I doubt you'll find many successful people who have not experienced this.

All successful people learn that success is buried on the other side of frustration. Unfortunately, some people don't get to the other side.

ANTHONY ROBBINS

Good ideas
and innovations
must be driven
into existence
by courageous patience.

ADMIRAL HYMAN RICKOVER

It is not the critic that counts;
not the man who points out how
the strong man stumbled or where
the doer of deeds could have done
them better. The credit belongs to
the man who is actually in the
arena; whose face is marred by
dust and sweat and blood; who
strives valiantly; who errs, and
comes short again and again,
because there is no effort without
error and shortcomings, who does
actually try to do the deed; who
knows the great enthusiasm, the
great devotion, and spends himself
in a worthy cause; who, at the worst,
if he fails, at least fails while
daring greatly.

CONT'D

Far better it is to dare mighty things, to win glorious triumphs even though checkered by failure, than to rank with those poor spirits who neither enjoy nor suffer much because they live in the gray twilight that know neither victory nor defeat.

THEODORE ROOSEVELT

Our doubts
are traitors,
and make us lose the good
we oft might win
by fearing
to attempt.

WILLIAM SHAKESPEARE

Here's a two-step formula for handling stress.

Step 1: Don't sweat the small stuff.

Step 2: Remember, it's all small stuff.

ANTHONY ROBBINS

創

The creative individual
not only respects the irrational
in himself, but courts the most
promising source of novelty in
his own thought...
The creative
person is both more primitive and
more cultured, more destructive
and more constructive, crazier
and saner, than the average person.

FRANK BARRON

行

Stop sitting there
   with your hands folded
      looking on,
         doing nothing;

Get into action
   and live this full
      and glorious life.

NOW.

      You have to do it.

EILEEN CADDY

Much is said in regard to 'building castles in the air', and one who is given to this building is not always looked upon with favour.

But castles in the air are always necessary before we can have castles on the ground, before we can have castles in which to live.

The trouble with the one who gives himself to building castles in the air is not that he builds them in the air, but that he does not go farther and actualise in life, in character, in material form, the castles he thus builds.

He does a part of the work, a very necessary part, but another equally necessary part remains still undone.

RALPH WALDO TRINE

To know
how to wait
is the great secret
of success.

JOSEPH DE MAISTRE

A good plan
violently executed
right now
is far better
than a perfect plan
executed
next week.

GENERAL GEORGE PATTON

The way you activate the seeds
of your creation is by making
choices about the results you want
to create.

When you make a choice, you
mobilise vast human energies and
resources which otherwise go
untapped.

All too often people fail to focus
their choices upon results and
therefore their choices are ineffect-
ive. If you limit your choices only
to what seems possible or reason-
able, you disconnect yourself
from what you truly want, and
all that is left is a compromise.

ROBERT FRITZ

A step in the wrong direction
is better than staying
on the spot all your life.

Once you're moving forward
you can correct
your course
as you go.

Your automatic
guidance system
cannot guide you
when you're
standing still.

MAXWELL MALTZ

伍

Live
Your beliefs
and you can turn
the World
around.

HENRY THOREAU

機

Many people sit around waiting for the world to discover them, and that rarely happens.

If you move toward your goals, expressing all your power, opportunity will find you as a result of your actions.

For by riding your energy, knowing and believing your higher Self is with you, you will be in the right place, at the right time.

But make the first move, taking constant care to purify and review your life; move from negative habits into the fortress of light.

Discipline is the horse you ride.

STUART WILDE

休

Take rest;

a field that has rested
gives a beautiful crop.

OVID

You are not here for any
destiny but to live, and in every
moment of living to do what the
creative self, the soul, urges you
to do. From that anything is
possible within the realms of
creation. You can create kingdoms
untold, lives untold. You can
fulfill yourself. You can become
whatever you desire to become
when you have allowed yourself
that explicit freedom.

And once you find out that
you are worth experiencing it all,
you can put forth your light into
any fulfillment that pleases you,
at any moment that pleases you.

RAMTHA

A lot of successful
people are risk-takers.

Unless you're willing to do that...
to have a go,
fail miserably,
and have another go,
success won't happen.

PHILLIP ADAMS

Analysis of several hundred people who had accumulated fortunes well beyond the million-dollar mark disclosed the fact that every one of them had the habit of reaching decisions promptly, and of changing these decisions slowly, if and when they were changed. People who fail to accumulate money, without exception, have the habit of reaching decisions very slowly, if at all, and of changing these decisions quickly and often.

NAPOLEON HILL

望

When everything
is going badly
and you are trying
to make up your mind,

look towards the heights,
no complications there.

CHARLES DE GAULLE

If a man
does not work
passionately
(even furiously)
at being the best in the world
at what he does,
he fails his talent,
his destiny
and his God.

GEORGE LOIS

The secret
of success
is making
your vocation
your vacation.

MARK TWAIN

how much longer will you go on
letting your energy sleep?

how much longer are you going
to stay oblivious of the
immensity of yourself?

Don't lose time in conflict;
lose no time in doubt —
Time can never be recovered,
and if you miss an opportunity
it may take many lives
before another comes
your way again.

BHAGWAN SHREE RAJNEESH

Begin with the possible;
begin with one step.
There is always a limit,
you cannot do more
than you can.

If you try to do too much,
you will do nothing.

P.D. OUSPENSKY
G.I. GURDJIEFF

Go confidently
in the direction of your dreams!
Live the life you've imagined.
As you simplify your life,
the laws of the universe
will be simpler;
Solitude will not be solitude,
Poverty will not be poverty,
nor weakness weakness.

HENRY DAVID THOREAU

The mind is the limit. As long as the mind can envision the fact that you can do something, you can do it - as long as you really believe 100 percent. It's all mind over matter.

All I know is that the first step is to create the vision, because when you see the vision there - the beautiful vision - that creates the 'want power. For example, my wanting to be Mr. Universe came about because I saw myself so clearly, being up there on the stage and winning.

ARNOLD SCHWARZENEGGER

It's a funny thing
about life;
if you refuse to accept
anything
but the best,
You very often get it.

W. SOMERSET MAUGHAM

They can
because
they think
they can.

VIRGIL

Nothing in the world can take the place of persistance. Talent will not; nothing is more common than unsuccessful men with talent. Genius will not; unrewarded genius is almost a proverb. Education alone will not; the world is full of educated derelicts. Persistance and determination alone are omnipotent.

CALVIN COOLIDGE

Why aren't we all empowered, happy, wealthy, healthy and successful? The truth is that even in the information age, information is not enough. If all we needed were ideas and positive thinking, then we all would have had ponies when we were kids and we would all be living our dream life now.

Action is what unites every great success. Action is what produces results. Knowledge is only potential power until it comes into the hands of someone who knows how to get himself to take effective action.

ANTHONY ROBBINS

A great deal of talent
is lost to the world for
want of a little courage.

Every day sends to their graves
obscure men whom timidity
prevented from making
a first effort.

SYDNEY SMITH

The real winners in life
are people who have developed
a strong positive 'self-expectancy'.
They have the ability to move in
the direction of the goals or
images they set, or roles they
want to play, and will tolerate
little distraction.

In the face of discouragement, mistakes, and setbacks,
this inner-drive or commitment
keeps them moving upward
toward self-fulfillment.

DENIS WAITLEY

There is
    only one success –
To be able to
    spend your life
        in your own way.

CHRISTOPHER MORLEY

励

Action is
is
eloquence.

WILLIAM SHAKESPEARE

You have to know
what you want to get.

But when you know that,
let it take you.

And if it seems to take you
off the track,
don't hold back,
because perhaps that is
instinctively where
you want to be.

And if you hold back
and try to be always where
you have been before,
you will go dry.

GERTRUDE STEIN

Where there
is no vision,
people perish.

PROVERBS 29:18

The thing has already taken form in my mind before I start it.

The first attempts are absolutely unbearable.

I say this because I want you to know that if you see something worthwhile in what I am doing, it is not by accident but because of real direction and purpose.

VINCENT VAN GOGH

$\mathcal{T}$here are no real
successes
without rejection.

$\mathcal{T}$he more rejection you get,
the better you are,
the more you've learned,
the closer you are
to your outcome.

ANTHONY ROBBINS

*T*he absence
of alternatives
clears the mind
marvellously.

HENRY KISSINGER

The human tendency toward the fossilizing of form is shocking, even tragic.

Yesterday the man who exhibited a new form was condemned.

Today the same form has become immovable law for all time.

This is tragic because it shows over and over again that human beings depend on externals.

WASSILY KANDINSKY

When you are inspired
by some great purpose,
some extraordinary project,
all your thoughts break their bonds;
Your mind transcends limitations,
your consciousness expands in
every direction, and you find yourself in a new, great and wonderful
world. Dormant forces, faculties
talents become alive, and you
discover yourself to be a greater
person by far than you ever
dreamed yourself
to be.

PATANJALI

The secret of making
something work in your lives,
is, first of all, the deep desire
to make it work:

Then the faith and belief
that it can work:

Then to hold that clear definite
vision in your consciousness
and see it working out
step by step, without one
thought of doubt
or disbelief.

EILEEN CADDY

The key is controlled urgency, treating every matter as something urgent to get done, and out of the way.

It means less time spent on useless conversation, less waiting patiently for someone else to move before you do, more action rather than putting things aside for later (whenever that is).

CHARLES H FORD

Things turn out best
for the people
who make the best
out of the way
things turn out.

ART LINKLETTER

的

Your automatic creative mechanism is teleological. That is, it operates in terms of goals and end results. Once you give it a definite goal to achieve you can depend upon its automatic guidance system to take you to that goal much better than 'You' ever could by conscious thought.

'You' supply the goal by thinking in terms of end results. Your automatic mechanism then supplies the 'means whereby'.

MAXWELL MALTZ

Learn the art of patience. Apply discipline to your thoughts when they become anxious over the outcome of a goal. Impatience breeds anxiety, fear, discouragement and failure.

Patience creates confidence, decisiveness and a rational outlook, which eventually leads to success.

BRIAN ADAMS

The greater the contrast,
the greater the potential.

Great energy
only comes
from a correspondingly
great tension
between opposites.

C G JUNG

So many people
go through life
without a direction.
They just go from stop to stop.
It's like they're on a bus
and the only time
they get off
is to piss.

TODD RUNDGREN

To be what we are,
and to become
what
we are capable
of becoming
is the only end of life.

R L STEVENSON

Positive self-expectancy is pure and simply optimism, in the face of all odds. Self-expectancy is the key to motivation. It begins where the self-image leaves off.

It takes the words, pictures and emotions of imagination, and fuses them into energy and action by commitment.

Winners have positive self-expectancy which creates desire. They are dissatisfied with the status quo. They want change for the better.

DENIS WAITLEY

The great
end of life
is not knowledge
but action.

THOMAS HENRY HUXLEY

Do the thing
and you will
have the
Power.

RALPH WALDO EMERSON

Emptiness is a symptom
that you are not living
creatively.

You either have no goal
that is important enough
to you, or you are not
using your talents and efforts
in striving toward
an important goal.

MAXWELL MALTZ

Things do not change;

We change.

HENRY DAVID THOREAU

智

For every cause, there will be an effect nearly equal in intensity.

If we make good use of our minds, skills and talents, these will become apparent in our outer lives.

And, if we make good use of our time, this too will give us a great advantage, for we know that scarcely one in a thousand individuals ever puts his or her time to anywhere near its potential good use. This is being true to ourselves - taking control, accepting responsibility. In the final analysis, we are the only ones from whom we can steal time and accomplishment.

EARL NIGHTINGALE

If I had to sum up in one word the qualities that make a good manager, I'd say that it all comes down to decisiveness. You can use the fanciest computers in the world and you can gather all the charts and numbers, but in the end you have to bring all your information together, set up a timetable, and act.

LEE IACOCCA

In terms of game theory, we might say the universe is so constituted as to maximise the play. The best games are not those in which all goes smoothly and steadily toward a certain conclusion, but those in which the outcome is always in doubt. Similarly, the geometry of life is designed to keep us at the point of maximum tension between certainty and uncertainty, order and chaos.

Every important call is a close one. We survive and evolve by the skin of our teeth. We really wouldn't want it any other way.

GEORGE LEONARD

Set me a task in which
  I can put something
    of myself,

and it is a task no longer;
    it is joy;
      it is art.

BLISS CARMEN

Never give in.

Never give in.

Never give in.

SIR WINSTON CHURCHILL

If you have built castles
in the air,
your work need not be lost;
that is where they should be.
Now put the foundations
under them.

HENRY DAVID THOREAU

Take your dream, attach it to a star and never lose it. If you lose it, you're a dead duck. You've lost your enthusiasm; you've settled for something less. This will never do. Fight like hell for your dream and get it. If you do, life will be a very beautiful, wonderful and exciting thing. You cannot compromise with people; you cannot compromise with yourself or you will sell yourself short. If you say, "I will not compromise in any way, shape or form; that is what I want, and I want that or nothing" you'll get it. You pay for it, yes; you get nothing for nothing.

GURU RHH

humans have learned only
through mistakes. The billions of
humans in history have had to make
quadrillions of mistakes to have
arrived at the state where we now
have 150,000 common words to
identify that many unique and
only metaphysically comprehensible
nuances of experience.

Chagrin and mortification
caused by their progressively self-
discovered quadrillions of errors
would long ago have given humanity such an inferiority complex
that it would have become too
discouraged to continue with the
life experience. To avoid such a
proclivity humans were designed-
ly given pride, vanity and invent-
ive memory, which, all together, can

CONT'D

and usually do incline us to self-deception.

...So effective has been the non-thinking, group deceit of humanity that it now says, "Nobody should make mistakes," and punishes people for making mistakes.

...The courage to adhere to the truth as we learn it involves, then, the courage to face ourselves, with the clear admission of all the mistakes we have made – mistakes are sins only when not admitted.

BUCKMINSTER FULLER

The truth is
that all of us
attain the greatest success
and happiness possible
in this life
whenever we use
our native capacities
to their greatest
extent.

DR SMILEY BLANTON

The great aim
of education
is not knowledge
but action.

HERBERT SPENCER

Some people have greatness
thrust upon them. Very few have
excellence thrust upon them....
They achieve it. They do not achieve
it unwittingly by doing what
comes naturally and they don't
stumble into it in the course of
amusing themselves. All excellence
involves discipline and tenacity
of purpose.

JOHN GARDNER

Whatever it is
however impossible it seems
Whatever the obstacle that lies
between you & it
If it is noble
If it is consistent
with God's Kingdom
You must hunger after it
and stretch yourself
to reach it.

CHARLES PAUL CONN

Life affords no higher
pleasure than that of surmounting
difficulties, passing from one step
of success to another, forming
new wishes and seeing
them gratified.

DR SAMUEL JOHNSON

While one person hesitates
because he feels inferior,
the other is busy making mistakes
and becoming superior.

HENRY C LINK

We are not in a position in which we have nothing to work with. We already have a start; we already have capacities, talents, direction, missions, callings.

The job is, if we are willing to take it seriously, to help ourselves to be more perfectly what we are, to be more full, more actualising, more realising, in fact, what we are in potentiality.

ABRAHAM MASLOW

Until you try,
    you don't know
        what you can't do.

HENRY JAMES

If you want to succeed
you should strike out
on new paths,
rather than travel the
worn paths
of accepted
success.

JOHN D ROCKEFELLER, SR

Perhaps the most valuable result of all education is the ability to make yourself do the thing you have to do when it ought to be done, whether you like it or not; it is the first lesson that ought to be learned; and however early a man's training begins, it is probably the last lesson that he learns thoroughly.

THOMAS HUXLEY

Nothing would be done
at all
if a man waited
until he could do it so well
that no-one could find
fault with it.

CARDINAL NEWMAN

You have in your
composition
a mighty genius
for expression
which has escaped
discipline.

HG WELLS

Nothing
comes from
doing
nothing.

WILLIAM SHAKESPEARE

We have been told in Scripture, we have seen demonstrated in psychology and have confirmed through bio-feedback and Kirlian photography that faith (belief) in one source, a knowledge of one power and one Omnipotent Creator is the great cornerstone of all power and all creative action.

The odds on successes and failures in and for life are established through our own consciousness; we make our luck or lack of it through only one means and that is our awareness and acceptance of the great I AM presence, the God within.

JACK HOLLAND

The great French Marshall Lyautey once asked his gardener to plant a tree. The gardener objected that the tree was slow growing and would not reach maturity for 100 years.

The Marshall replied, "In that case, there is no time to lose; plant it this afternoon".

J F KENNEDY

Don't refuse
    to go on an occasional
        wild goose chase.
That's what wild geese are for.

ANON

Often people attempt to live
their lives backwards; they try to
have more things, or more money,
in order to do more of what they
want, so they will be happier.

The way it actually works is
the reverse. You must first be who
you really are, then do what you
need to do, in order to have what
you want.

MARGARET YOUNG

Men stumble over the truth
from time to time,
but most pick themselves up
and hurry off
as if nothing
happened.

SIR WINSTON CHURCHILL

Unless you put the house of your life - the physical and verbal structures - in order, the urge for exploration of that which is beyond time and space will remain only a wish in the mind.

If there is disorder in simple things of life like diet, sleep, exercise, breathing, trying to build a structure of exploration will be like building a house in the sand.

VIMALA THAKAR

A crank
    is a man
        with a new idea -
until it catches on.

MARK TWAIN

This art
of resting the mind
and the power
of dismissing from it
all care and worry
is probably one of the
secrets of energy
in our great men.

CAPT J A HADFIELD

Perhaps what we call genius has something to do with a learned state of consciousness, a way of attending to the stream of mental experience. Perhaps many more of us could hear inner melodies, find guidance and inspiration, achieve breakthrough insight – if we would only pay more atten- tion to the fleeting images and the quiet intuitions presented to us by the creative mind.

WILLIS HARMEN

People are always fixated at lower levels. Self-actualisation is the tendency of every human being to make real his or her full potential, to become everything that he or she can be.

The self-actualising person is the true human-specied-type.... not a normal person with something added, but a normal person with nothing taken away.

ABRAHAM MASLOW

What's really important in life? Sitting on the beach? Looking at television eight hours a day? I think we have to appreciate that we're alive for only a limited period of time, and we'll spend most of our lives working. That being the case, I believe one of the most important priorities is to do whatever we do as well as we can. We should take pride in that.

VICTOR KIAM

Two dejected assistants of
Thomas Edison said:
    "We've just completed our seven
hundredth experiment and we still
don't have the answer. We have
failed."

    "No, my friends, you haven't
failed" replied Mr. Edison. "It's just
that we know more about this
subject than anyone else alive. And
we're closer to finding the answer,
because now we know seven hundred
things not to do. Don't call it a
mistake. Call it an education."

The winners edge
in self-dimension is to
have a worthy destination
and look beyond yourself for
meaning in life. The greatest example of self-dimension a winner can
display is the quality of earning
the love and respect of other human
beings. Winners create other winners without exploiting them. They
know that true immortality for
the human race is when a
caring, sharing person
helps even one other
individual.

DENIS WAITLEY

You will have
wonderful surges
forward.

Then there must be
a time of consolidating
before the next
forward surge.

Accept this
as part of the process
and never become
downhearted.

EILEEN CADDY

Never feel guilty
about learning.
Never feel guilty
about wisdom.
That is called enlightenment.

You must understand that you
have done what you needed
to do; it was all necessary.

And you made all the right
choices - all of them!

RAMTHA

弱

Failure
is often
the line
of least persistance.

ZIG ZIGLAR

Every kind of work can be a pleasure. Even simple household tasks can be an opportunity to exercise and expand our caring, our effectiveness, our responsiveness.

As we respond with caring and vision to all work, we develop our capacity to respond fully to all of life. Every action generates the energy which can be shared with others. These qualities of caring and responsiveness are the greatest gift we can offer.

TARTHANG TULKU

In the orientation of the creative you are naturally and easily able to build momentum. Every action you take, whether it is directly successful or not, adds additional energy to your path.

Because of this, everything you do works towards creating eventual success, including those things which are not immediately successful.

Over a period of time, creating the results you want gets easier and easier.

ROBERT FRITZ

Decide what you want,
decide what you are willing
to exchange for it.
Establish your priorities
and go to work.

H L HUNT

Life is constantly
providing us
with new funds,
new resources,
even when we are reduced
to immobility.

In life's ledger
there is no such thing
as frozen assets.

HENRY MILLER

Action
  springs
    not from thought,
but from
  a readiness
    for responsibility.

DIETRICH BONHOEFFER

Always leave enough time
in your life to do something
that makes you happy,
satisfied, or even joyous.

That has more of an effect
on economic well-being
than any other
single factor.

PAUL HAWKEN

The greatest pleasure
in life
is doing
what people say
you cannot do.

WALTER BAGEHOT

There is no heavier burden
than a
great potential.

CHARLIE BROWN

Don't cling to the
things of the past,
rejecting new concepts
and new challenges.

This negative mental attitude
blocks the creative processes
from true expression
causing mental inertia,
which is to live
in a vacuum,
to mentally wither
and die on the vine.

BRIAN ADAMS

The action of the child
inventing a new game with his
playmates;
        Einstein formulating a
theory of relativity;
        the housewife devising a
new sauce for the meat,
        a young author writing his
first novel;
        all of these are in terms of
definition, Creative, and there
is no attempt to set them in some
order of more or less Creative.

CARL R ROGERS

Intelligence
 highly awakened
 is intuition
 which is the only
 true guide in life.

KRISHNAMURTI

Business should be fun.
Without fun, people are left wearing emotional raincoats most of their working lives. Building fun into business is vital; it brings life into our daily being.

Fun is a powerful motive for most of our activities and should be a direct path of our livelihood. We should not relegate it to something we buy after work with money we earn.

MICHAEL PHILLIPS

The longer I live, the more importance I attach to a man's ability to manage and discipline himself... The man with the capacity for self-discipline can tell himself to do the truly important things first. Therefore, if there is not enough time to go around and something must be neglected, it will be the less essential task.

Here is the most interesting thing about the capacity for self-discipline, he who wants it may have it!... The one ingredient we most need for success is ours for the asking, for the wanting, if we only want it enough!

RAY KROC

When I was a young man
I observed that nine out of ten
things I did were failures.

I didn't want to be
a failure,
so I did ten times more work.

GEORGE BERNARD SHAW

Life is not a situation, but a process; not static, but dynamic. It's essential element is change, and the great question facing each of us is whether we will channel that change in the directions we want to go, shaping our destiny, or whether we will permit our activities and our character to be determined by those random forces we call fate. To the extent that we procrastinate, we are following the second course.

EDWIN C BLISS

If you don't follow through on your creative ideas, someone else will pick them up and use them. When you get an idea of this sort, you should jump in with both feet, not just stick your toe in the water...

Be daring, be fearless, and don't be afraid that somebody is going to criticize you or laugh at you. If your ego is not involved no one can hurt you.

GURU R.H.H.

Commit yourself to a dream. You affirm you're created in the image of God, that you have latent abilities, that you deserve to succeed as much as anybody else, and after you begin to believe that somehow, some way, somewhere, some time, through someone, you can make it.

When you are inspired with a dream, God has hit the ball into your court. Now you have to hit it back with a commitment.

ROBERT H SCHULLER

Most men would feel
insulted if it were proposed to
employ them in throwing stones
over a wall, and then throwing
them back merely that they might
earn their wages. But many
are no more worthily
employed now.

HENRY D THOREAU

If an unusual necessity forces us onward, a surprising thing occurs. The fatigue gets worse up to a certain point, when, gradually or suddenly, it passes away and we are fresher than before! We have evidently tapped a new level of energy. There may be layer after layer of this experience, a third and fourth "wind.

We find amounts of ease and power that we never dreamed ourselves to own, sources of strength habitually not taxed, because habitually we never push through the obstruction of fatigue.

WILLIAM JAMES

質

...He takes whatever dull job he's stuck with...and just to keep himself amused, starts to look for options of Quality, and secretly pursues these options, just for their own sake, thus making art out of what he is doing, he's likely to discover that he becomes a much more interesting person and much less of an object to the people around him because his Quality decisions change him too. And not only the job and him, but others too because the Quality tends to fan out like waves. The Quality job he didn't think anyone was going to see is seen, and the person who sees it feels a little better of it, and is likely to pass that feeling onto others, and in that way the Quality tends to keep on going.

ROBERT PIRSIG

...Know what you are going to do and then do it and don't backslide. If you make a mistake, make a glorious one. It's like the man who comes to the tree at the fork in the road and says, "Which way shall I go, this way or that?"

Go! Take one way and go. There is always the element of timing. Everything has a time and place.

GURU RHH

Transcendence is the power to be born anew, to make a fresh start, to turn over a new leaf, to begin with a clean slate, to enter into a state of grace, to have a second chance.

Transcendence makes no reference to the past, whether your past has been overflowing with victories or filled with defeats. When you enter a state of transcendence you are able to create a new life, unburdened by both the victories and the defeats of the past.

Transcendence is more than just the accurate realization that the past is over. It is also a realignment of all dimensions of yourself with the very source of your life.

ROBERT FRITZ

Man
cannot discover
new oceans
Until he has courage
to lose sight
of the shore.

ANON

Limitation has been an adventure; it has been an experience, and most on this plane are experiencing it, greatly. Unfortunately, you forgot that there is something better and you made limitation a way of life! If you only knew that through unlimited thinking you transcend the embodiment, and all universes and planes, you would never choose to be limited again.

If you only knew that and allowed yourself to receive and embrace all thoughts, you would have joy and peace in life beyond your grandest dreams.

RAMTHA

Life's fulfillment finds constant contradictions in its path; but those are necessary for the sake of its advance.

The stream is saved from the sluggishness of its current by the perpetual opposition of the soil through which it must cut its way. It is the soil which form its banks.

The Spirit of fight belongs to the genius of life.

RABINDRANATH TAGORE

Set your sights high,
the higher the better.

Expect the most wonderful
things to happen,
not in the future
but right now.

Realise that nothing
is too good.

Allow absolutely nothing
to hamper you
or hold you up
in any way.

EILEEN CADDY

The real dividing line
between the things
we call work
and the things we call leisure
is that in leisure,
however active we may be,
we make our own choices
and our own decisions.

We feel for the time being
that our life
is our own.

RAYMOND WILLIAMS

If you do
what you've always done,

You'll get
what you've always gotten.

ANON

Your potential is unlimited.
Aspire to a high place.
Believe in your abilities,
in your tastes,
in your own judgement.

Image and perceive
that which you wish to be.
Back your image with
enthusiasm and courage.

Feel the reality of your 'new'
self; live in the expectancy
of greater things and your
subconscious will
actualise them.

BRIAN ADAMS

To change one's life;

: Start immediately
: Do it flamboyantly
: No exceptions

WILLIAM JAMES

Winning
starts with
Beginning.

ROBERT SCHULLER

BIBLIOGRAPHY

The author would like to thank the following authors and publishers for permission to reprint material from their books:

Adams, Brian. *How To Succeed* , Copyright ©1985 by Brian Adams. Published by Melvin Powers Wilshire Book Company, California. Used by Permission.

Caddy, Eileen. *Footprints On The Path; God Spoke To Me*, Copyright © 1971, 1976 Findhorn Press, The Park, Forres, Scotland. Used by Permission.

Fritz, Robert. *The Path of Least Resistance*, Copyright © 1984 by Robert Fritz. Published by DMA, Inc., 9 Pickering Way, Salem, MA 01970.

Green, Renie. *Who Said That*, Copyright © Renie Green 1984. Published by David & Charles Publishers, Brunel House, Newton Abbot, Devon. Used by Permission.

Maltz M.D., Maxwell. *Psycho-Cybernetics*, Copyright © 1960 by Prentice-Hall, Inc., Englewood Cliffs, N.J.

Pirsig, Robert M., *Zen And The Art of Motor Cycle Maintenance*, Copyright © 1974 by Robert M. Pirsig. Used by Permission of the Publisher, The Bodley Head, 32 Bedford Square, London WC1.

Ramtha, Copyright © 1986 by Sovereignty, Inc., Box 909 Eastsound, Washington. Used by Permission.

Robbins, Anthony. *Unlimited Power*, Copyright © 1986 by Anthony Robbins. Reprinted by permission of Simon & Schuster, Inc., 1230 Avenue of the Americas, New York.

Talk Does Not Cook The Rice, Series 2 - A Commentary on the Teaching of Agni Yoga by Guru R.H.H., Copyright © 1985 Foundations of Culture. Reprinted by permission of Samuel Weiser, Inc., York Beach, Maine.

Trine, Ralph Waldo. *TWO By Ralph Waldo Trine, In Tune With The Infinite.* Special Contents Copyright © 1986 by Keats Publishing, Inc. Reprinted by permission of Keats Publishing, Inc. C.T., USA.

Waitley, Denis. *The Winner's Edge*, Copyright © 1980 by Denis Waitley. Published by Times Books, A Division of Random House, Inc. 201 East 50th Street, New York.

Wilde, Stuart. *The Force*, Copyright © 1984 by Stuart Wilde. Published by Wisdom Books, Inc., Taos, New Mexico. Used by Permission.

OTHER SOURCES AND RECOMMENDED READING;

The Bible, King James Version.

Bliss, Edwin C. *Doing It Now.* Futura Publications, A Division of Macdonald & Co. (Publishers) Ltd, 1984.

Chop Wood Carry Water - A Guide to Finding Spiritual Fulfillment in Everyday Life by Rick Fields with Peggy Taylor, Rex Weyler, and Rick Ingrasci: Jeremy P. Tarcher, Inc., Los Angeles, CA., 1984.

Gardner, John W. *Excellence: Can We Be Equal & Excellent Too.* New York: Harper & Row Publishers, Inc. 1961; Harper & Row Publishers Inc., Perennial Library, 1971, paperback.

Goethe, Johann Wolfgang von. *Faust: A Tragedy,* Translated in the original meters by Bayard Taylor, New York, Random House, 1967 (Modern Library).

Green, Jonathon. *Morrow's International Dictionary Of Contemporary Quotations.* William Morrow & Co. Inc., 105 Madison Ave, New York, 1982.

Hadfield, J. A. *The Psychology of Power,* The Macmillan Co., 866 Third Avenue, New York, 1919.

Harman Ph.D, Willis and Howard Rheingold. *Higher Creativity: Liberating the Unconscious for Breakthrough Insights.* Los Angeles: Jeremy P. Tarcher, Inc. CA.

Hill, Napoleon. *Think and Grow Rich.* New York: Hawthorne Books, Inc., 1966: Fawcett World Library, 1976, paperback.

Iacocca, Lee. *Iacocca, An Autobiography.* Bantam Books, Inc., 666 Fifth Avenue, New York; 1984.

James, William. *The Energies of Men,* from Memories and Studies. New York: Longmans, Green & Co., 1911.

Johnstone, Valerie. *Secrets of Success,* Night Owl Publishers Pty Ltd, Shepparton, VIC., 1985.

Lao Tzu, *Tao Te Ching, A New Translation* by Gia-Fu Feng and Jane English: Viking Press, 1972.

Leonard, George. *The Silent Pulse,* Wildwood House Ltd, London, 1978.

Maslow, Abraham H. *The Farther Reaches of Human Nature,* New York: Viking Press, Inc., 1971. *Toward A Psychology of Being,* Van Nostrand, 1962.

Meditations of Marcus Aurelius, translated by George Long, Mount Vernon, N.Y. Peter Pauper Press.

Murray, W. H. *The Scottish Himalayan Expedition*, Copyright ©
1951, Published by J. H. Dent & Sons Ltd.

Nightingale, Earl. *This is Earl Nightingale*, Doubleday & Co. Inc.,
New York, 1969.

Phillips, Michael and Rasberry, Salli. *Honest Business*, Random
House, 1981.

Rogers, Carl R. *On Becoming A Person: A Therapist's View of
Psychotherapy*, Constable & Company Ltd, London 1967.

Russell, Bertrand. *The Conquest of Happiness*, George Allen &
Unwin (Publishers) Ltd, 1930. Unwin Paperbacks, 1985.

Schuller, Dr. Robert H. *Tough Times Never Last, But Tough
People Do!* Thomas Nelson, Inc., Nashville TN., Bantam Books
Edition, June 1984.

Seth Speaks: The Eternal Validity of the Soul by Jane Roberts.
Prentice-Hall International, Inc. London 1972.

Shakespeare, William. *Complete Works*, Cambridge Text
established by John Denver Wilson, London: Octopus 1983.

Tagore, Dr. Rabindranath. *Glorious Thoughts of Tagore*, New
Book Society of India, 1965.

Tarthang Tulku, *Skillful Means*, Dharma Publishing, 1978.

Thakar, Vimala. *The Eloquence of Living*, Vimala Programs,
Berkeley, CA, 1981.

Thoreau, Henry David. *Walden* (Modern Library Edition).

Ziglar, Zig. *Steps To The Top*, Pelican Publishing Co. 1985.

While every effort has been made to acknowledge all copyright
holders, we apologise if any omissions have been made. Please
notify the publisher if this has occurred.

About the author

Originally from New Zealand, Susan Hayward now lives and operates her publishing company in Palm Beach, Australia. She is married with two children.

Please visit our website:
www.haywardbooks.com.au